Straphanging in the USA
Trolleys and Subways in American Life

Transportation
in America

Straphanging in the USA
Trolleys and Subways in American Life

Martin W. Sandler

OXFORD
UNIVERSITY PRESS

*This book is dedicated to Zelma Miller,
my aunt and friend, who introduced me to
the joys of riding the trolley.*

OXFORD
UNIVERSITY PRESS

Oxford   New York
Auckland   Bangkok   Buenos Aires   Cape Town   Chennai
Dar es Salaam   Delhi   Hong Kong   Istanbul   Karachi   Kolkata
Kuala Lumpur   Madrid   Melbourne   Mexico City   Mumbai   Nairobi
São Paulo   Shanghai   Singapore   Taipei   Tokyo   Toronto

Copyright © 2003 by Martin W. Sandler

Design by Alexis Siroc

Published by Oxford University Press, Inc.
198 Madison Avenue, New York, New York 10016
http://www.oup-usa.org

Oxford is a registered trademark of Oxford University Press

Library of Congress Cataloging-in-Publication Data

Sandler, Martin W.
  Straphanging in the USA : trolleys and subways in American life /
  Martin W. Sandler.
    p. cm. — (Transportation in America)
Summary: An illustrated look at how the problem of moving large numbers of
people within cities has been addressed through a series of vehicles and systems,
from horse-drawn cars to the modern subway.
Includes bibliographical references and index.
  ISBN 0-19-513229-7 (alk. paper)
  1. Street-railroads—United States—History. 2. Subways—United States—History.
  3. Trolley cars—United States—History. 4. Urban transportation—United States—
History. [1. Street-railroads. 2. Subways. 3. Trolley cars. 4. Urban transportation.
  5. Transportation. 6. City and town life.] I. Title. II. Series.
  HE4451 .S26 2003
    388.4'2'0973—dc21   2002014157

9 8 7 6 5 4 3 2 1

Printed in Hong Kong on acid-free paper

ON THE COVER: **A late 19th-century electric trolley makes
its way along the Mount Lowe Railway overlooking
Los Angeles.**

FRONTISPIECE: **Trolleys travel down a New York City street
in *The Bowery at Night,* painted in 1895.**

Contents

CHAPTER 1
Horsecars, Els, and Cable Cars

"*This event will go down in the history of our country as the greatest achievement of man.*"

—New York City Mayor Walter Browne
on the opening of the nation's first horsecar line, 1832

Americans have always been searching for new and better ways of moving around. The shrill blast of the steamboat, the haunting whistle of the train, the loud honk of an automobile horn have all symbolized different eras of transportation. One of the most distinctive and common sounds of the past was the clang of a trolley bell. For more than 50 years, trolleys, in one form or another, carried people to work, to amusement parks and suburbs, and to destinations both near and far. It may be hard to imagine, but there was a time when millions of Americans traveled by trolley every year.

The trolley was born in the city, at a time when the growth of urban areas in America was astounding. The figures tell the story. In 1890 there were 12 times as many people living in the United States as there had been in 1800. But the urban population of the United States in 1890 was 87 times greater than it had been at the start of the century. As cities became increasingly crowded, finding a way to transport people became a pressing issue. Out of this need came a horse-drawn vehicle called an omnibus (which comes from the Latin word *omnis,* meaning "all").

The first omnibus line in the United States—and the nation's first urban public transportation system—was established by Abraham Brower in New York City in 1831. This line became so popular that, within four years, more than 100 omnibuses were making their way up and down the streets of New York. By 1844, Boston, Philadelphia, and Baltimore all had their own omnibus lines.

The earliest omnibuses, with their oval-shaped bodies, looked very much like stagecoaches, but it was not long before they were redesigned with longer carriages that were more buslike. Pulled along by a team of two to six horses, each of the vehicles featured wide, curtained windows and had the word *Omnibus* painted on both sides. Like stagecoaches, many of the buses were named for prominent Americans and had brightly colored scenes painted on their sides as well.

The entrance to the omnibus was at the back of the vehicle, and in the earliest days, passengers paid their fares to a young boy who stood on the rear platform. It was not long, however, before these boys were replaced

The horse-drawn omnibus gave Americans their first form of public transportation. They also introduced city dwellers to traffic jams such as this one in New York.

by a fare-collection box mounted next to the driver. Before a more sophisticated braking system was adopted, omnibuses were halted by a most novel method. A strap connected to the rear door ran the length of the vehicle and was attached to the driver's leg. When a passenger opened the door, signaling the desire to disembark, the strap pulled at the driver's leg. Once the

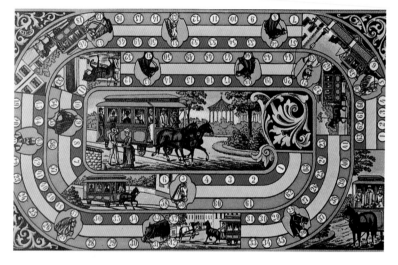

Eager to capitalize on the popularity of the horsecar, manufacturers created horsecar-themed toys and games. In this game, players roll dice and move their tokens to reach a particular destination on the board.

door was closed, the strap slackened, letting the driver know that he could start up again.

Although the omnibuses provided city dwellers with the best form of urban mass transit yet devised, they presented many problems of both comfort and safety. As the vehicles traveled along the uneven and sometimes cobblestoned streets, passengers in the overcrowded vehicles were jostled about, often banging into one another. Drivers, anxious to gather as many fares as they could, raced against buses from rival lines in order to be the first to reach waiting passengers. Accidents resulted, and every year scores of passengers, pedestrians, and drivers hauling other types of wagons were injured and even killed. "A ferocious spirit appears to have taken possession of the drivers, which defies law and delights in destruction," exclaimed the *Philadelphia Sunday Dispatch* in 1853.

Despite the chaos caused by omnibus traffic, city dwellers appreciated the benefits of public transportation. Transit owners soon developed the horsecar, a more comfortable and less dangerous method of moving

The introduction of electric street lamps in the early 1880s made it possible for horsecars, such as this one in Indianapolis, to move along city streets after dark. It was also electricity that led to the introduction of the horsecar's successor, the trolley.

people around. Although they were more elaborately decorated, horsecars looked a lot like omnibuses. The significant difference was that horsecars were hauled along rails set into city streets rather than pulled haphazardly. The horsecar utilized the same type of rails as the railroads, which were just beginning to appear on the American landscape in the 1830s. Traveling on rails along a set route provided passengers with a much smoother and more reliable ride.

The nation's first horsecar line was established in New York in 1832 by John Mason, one of the city's leading businessmen. By 1860, there were bustling horsecar lines in Chicago, Cincinnati, Pittsburgh, Boston, Baltimore, and Philadelphia. By 1880, there were 415 horsecar companies operating on some 3,000 miles of track, throughout the United States. In that year alone, more than 25 million passengers traveled by horsecar.

Yet, for all the riders they attracted, horsecar lines did not generate great profits for their owners. Each horsecar line depended, above all else, on horses. And the strong, agile, clever horses that were needed to pull the cars through chaotic city traffic were expensive. In addition, the strain of pulling the passenger-filled cars took a heavy physical toll on the animals, limiting their service to from three to five years. In 1872 a crisis occurred when a devastating horse disease, known as the Great Epizootic, spread throughout eastern cities. Thousands of animals died and thousands more were disabled. Many horsecar lines had to suspend operations, while others were able to continue only by hiring gangs of men to pull the cars through the streets by hand.

Increasingly, it became apparent that cities needed a transportation system that was not dependent upon animal power. Even when the animals were healthy, the congested street traffic was chaotic and dangerous. "Something more than streetcars and omnibuses is needed to supply the popular demand for city conveyance," claimed the *New York Herald* in 1864. "It must be evident to everybody that neither the cars nor the omnibuses supply accommodations enough for the public, and such accommodations as they do supply are not of the right sort."

Its cars were noisy and its tracks blocked the sun from city streets, but the El soon became an important part of life in many cities. As one Chicago resident wrote in a letter to the editor of the *Chicago Sun Times*, "Riding the elevated gives me a better chance to see my city than any other way."

railway. It was a system of tracks supported by tall steel girders that rose above the city streets. By 1868, the first section of New

Actually, a whole new kind of urban transportation designed to relieve street congestion was already under construction some seven years before the Great Epizootic struck. In New York City, a company established by Charles Harvey had begun to erect what would eventually become the nation's first elevated York's El, as it came to be called, was completed. The elevated cars were pulled by stubby steam locomotives that traveled three times faster than horsecars. "The rapid speed attained leaves friends of the enterprise to hope that the problem of rapid and safe locomotion through the crowded streets of the city has been satisfied,"

Andrew Hallidie's cable car system was a bold new idea in city transportation. This diagram shows how the cable, located in a pipe under the street, was attached to the grip that controlled the car.

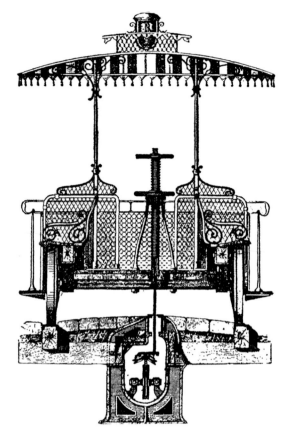

reported a correspondent for *Harper's Weekly* who was among the first to ride on Harvey's cars.

Constructing an elevated railway system was an enormously expensive undertaking, and despite its initial success, Charles Harvey's company went broke. Other companies, however, picked up the work, and from the 1870s to the early 1900s, elevated lines spread throughout New York. By the mid 1880s, tens of thousands of passengers were riding the New York El every day. Motivated by this success, other cities, most notably Boston and Chicago, constructed their own elevated railway systems.

Elevated railways certainly helped relieve congestion on city streets, but even at the height of their popularity, they, too, presented problems. The elevated trains blocked out the sky and the sun and turned the streets below into dark, foreboding areas. The cars rattling across the overhead rails created an incessant racket. Still, the elevated railways represented one of the first effective attempts to bring more efficient rapid transit to the city. It was, in fact, not until the mid-1950s that many cities began to remove their Els.

The elevated railway was not the only new type of urban transportation that was introduced in an attempt to improve upon the omnibus and horsecar. In 1873, Andrew Hallidie, a manufacturer of wire ropes called cables, introduced his cable railway in San Francisco. Hallidie drew inspiration for the system from England, where coal cars were commonly hauled to and from the mines by cable. At a central facility, Hallidie installed a steam engine, which powered an endless cable that ran continuously and slid over rollers in an underground trench. A grip attached to the underside of the cable car enabled the driver, called a gripman, to snare or release the moving cable, allowing the car to stop and start, and to move along at a desired speed.

The cable car was an instant success. Not only did it eliminate the need for horses, but it traveled at 9 or 10 miles an hour, about double the speed of a horsecar. It could climb and descend hills with ease. San Francisco almost immediately built other cable car lines, and Chicago, Philadelphia, and other cities followed suit. In New York, a cable line was constructed along the newly built Brooklyn Bridge. Within a year, this one line carried more than 9 million passengers.

By 1894, cable cars were in operation from Washington, D.C., to Denver, Colorado, transporting some 400 million passengers a year. But, like the elevated lines, the cable systems had serious drawbacks. They were expensive to install. The complexity of their machinery made them prone to breakdowns. And, even though no one could know it at the time, one of the century's most important inventions would limit the cable car's popularity. While Hallidie and others were introducing and perfecting their systems, other inventors were developing ways to put newly harnessed electricity to work in transportation. The electric trolley would soon appear in American cities.

Sizes and Shapes of Horsecars

The yellow belly. Like an omnibus, this type of horsecar had a low side panel that curved inward and an upper panel that curved outward to provide more space inside the car. It got its name from the fact that the lower panel was usually painted a bright yellow.

The bob-tail. This car had a single step in the rear rather than a platform and got its name from the fact that the step bobbed up and down as the car moved.

The balloon car. Unlike some horsecars that were turned around by means of a turntable at the end of the railway line, this short, stubby car swiveled around by itself.

The double-decker. The winding stairway at one end of this car enabled passengers to climb to an upper level for a better view of the city.

The double-ender. This car had both a front and a rear platform. Cigar-smoking passengers stood on the rear platform while the reins-holding driver stood on the front. The double-ender eliminated the need for cars to turn around when making a return trip.

The convertible. In the warm-weather months the wooden panels on the sides of this car were removed so that passengers could enjoy the summer breezes.

The double-decker was a particularly popular form of horsecar. Along with increasing the number of riders that could be carried, the upper deck gave passengers an unobstructed view of the city.

CHAPTER 2

Trolley Mania

"To the already deafening clamor of our cities, a new sound has been added. The constant, clattering clang of the trolley."

—*Milwaukee Eagle*, 1873

In 1831, English scientist Michael Faraday discovered that electricity could be used to power machinery, and the seeds for the invention of the electric trolley were planted. Between 1835 and 1851, several inventors—notably Robert Davidson in Scotland and Thomas Davenport, Moses Farmer, and Charles Page in the United States—developed battery-powered motors that successfully drove trolley cars over a short distance. Their achievements represented a major breakthrough, but the crude batteries available at the time were unreliable and costly. Electric generators would have to be developed before transportation by electric power could become a practical reality.

By the 1880s, a number of inventors had discovered how to build such generators. In 1884 Edward M. Bentley and Walter H. Knight devised a primitive system of supplying electric power to the Cleveland street railway system, and the stage was set for the full development of the trolley.

This pivotal advancement in the history of transportation was accomplished by an engineer named Frank J. Sprague. A native of Milford, Connecticut,

Electricity paved the way for inventors to create various types of trolleys. This open-sided vehicle provided passengers spectacular views of the scenery around Los Angeles from the elevated tracks.

Sprague had become fascinated with the potential of electricity while a midshipman at the U.S. Naval Academy. In the years immediately following his graduation, he served tours of duty on two different vessels. While aboard them, he produced some 60 inventions, including a system for installing incandescent lights on ships and a unique type of electric dynamo. By 1883

Sprague was devoting much of his free time to considering ways in which electric power could be applied to street railways. He resigned from the navy and went to work as an assistant to the inventor Thomas Edison, where he further developed his ideas. A year later, he left Edison's laboratories to form his own company.

Over the next five years, Sprague concentrated on solving the problems that the early electric street-railway pioneers had been unable to overcome. Earlier experimenters, for example, had tried various methods, including belts and chains, of mounting the motor to the vehicle. Repeated breakdowns and loss of power were the result. Sprague solved these prob-

ORANGE EMPIRE
TROLLEY TRIP

Through California's
Orange Kingdom
Operates
Wednesdays and Sundays
9: A.M.

PACIFIC ELECTRIC RAILWAY
LOS ANGELES / CALIFORNIA

In order to attract business, trolley companies ran excursions through scenic areas. This brochure describes the sites on a trip through California's Orange County.

lems by mounting the motor directly on the car's axle through the use of specially constructed gears.

Sprague's greatest innovation, however, was the development of the first efficient system of supplying electricity to the motor. His predecessors had powered the motors by electrifying one of the rails upon which the cars traveled. Sprague's system supplied electric current directly to the motors through overhead wires. Sprague's cars were connected to the wires by a pole that each car had mounted on its roof. A grooved wheel at the top of the pole pressed against the overhead wire and transferred electric power to the car. The wheel was known as a troller, and from this device the trolley got its name.

News of Sprague's accomplishments soon spread, and early in 1887 he obtained a contract from the city of Richmond, Virginia, for the construction of a new, electrically powered street railway system. By January 1888, Sprague's company was operating nine trolleys throughout that city. A report in the *Richmond Whig* extolled the virtues of the new system and claimed that the only difficulties occurred when youngsters played pranks by putting rocks on the trolley tracks.

By the middle of 1888, 40 of Sprague's trolleys were traveling the streets of Richmond. Passengers were delighted, which was not surprising, because the trolley had obvious advantages over the omnibus, the horse-car, and the cable systems. Electric power enabled the trolley to accelerate rapidly and to travel more than five times faster than omnibuses or horsecars. Eliminating horses as a power source meant the disappearance of tons of manure that the animals had dumped on the city streets each year, which was both a nuisance and a health threat. And trolleys could carry far more passengers than any previous form of urban transit. Thanks to yet another Frank Sprague invention—a system of linking the electric car controls of several railway cars—two or more cars could be coupled together and operated safely.

Within three months of its opening, Richmond's trolley system was transporting some 12,000 passengers a day. The system captured such instant national acclaim and represented so monumental a transportation breakthrough that only two years after Sprague's trolleys made their debut, more than 200 electric street railway systems were operating throughout the United States. It was the beginning of a period of more than 30 years that some transportation historians have called the "era of trolley mania," one in which almost every city and town in the nation had a bustling trolley system.

Onlookers watch the trolley as it moves trough New Orleans's historic French Quarter. By the mid-1890s, almost every city in America had its own trolley system.

Being a trolley motorman was an enjoyable job. "You see the sunshine and the flowers," stated a motorman's handbook. "You are out among people and have an idea of what the world is doing."

A typical trolley was operated by a motorman, who drove the vehicle, and a conductor, who collected fares, punched tickets, and issued transfers. The conductor had other jobs as well. When the trolley came to a turnout, he would grab a heavy iron bar and use it to turn a switch in the tracks that would head the trolley in the desired direction. When the trolley reached the end of its line, it was also the conductor's job to loosen the rope that held the pole to the overhead wires and to swing the pole over to the other end of the car so that the trolley could continue its run in the opposite direction.

Many regular passengers came to know the conductors by name, but it was the motormen who were generally more popular. The omnibus and horsecar drivers were mostly unfriendly and often had poor personal hygiene. The trolley motormen, however, were trained to be polite and well groomed. As trolley companies grew, the larger ones published pamphlets and handbooks regulating the motorman's behavior and appearance.

"Don't lose your temper!" advised the editor of a pamphlet published by the Chicago Trolley Company in 1904:

> Many a motorman has lost his position because of a quick temper. I remember a motorman who was always ill-tempered. The minute he got his hands on the controls, he was angry at everything and everyone. The conductor was too slow, or too many people were riding. I personally know of one accident he was entirely to blame for because of his temper. Do not forget your personal appearance. Nothing gives a motorman a better stand in the public eye than to be clean and neatly dressed. If there is anything that disgusts me, it is to sit behind a motorman and gaze on a neck so dirty that you could raise a crop of potatoes on it.

The trolley companies established rules for passengers as well as for their employees. Accustomed to the much slower pace of the horsecars, riders were apt to jump aboard a trolley before it stopped. Early on, many passengers were injured when they misjudged the speed of the vehicle. Trolley companies therefore posted signs showing how to get on and off a car.

All of these rules became increasingly important as the trolley continued to dominate the landscape of the city. Before its glory days were over, the trolley would change the way of life of the entire nation as well.

Millions of Americans rode the trolleys just for the sheer joy of it. Trolley companies ran special decorated cars like this one in Philadelphia, complete with bands, entertainers, refreshments, and lots of lights.

CHAPTER 3

The Trolley Changes America

"The trolley is changing America, but nowhere more than the manner in which it is moving [people] from country to city and back again."

—*The New York Times*, 1893

Unlike the earlier transportation companies, the trolley companies were enormously profitable almost from the beginning. This was largely thanks to their ability to carry so many passengers and to the efficiency of electric power. But the trolley companies added to their financial success by continually developing new ideas and designing new attractions aimed at luring even greater numbers of passengers to their lines.

The trolley appeared at a time when the six- or even seven-day workweek was beginning to shrink. Increasingly, Sunday was accepted as the workman's holiday. Trolley companies seized the opportunity to convince people to take the trolley out of the city on their day off.

The companies built scores of attractions throughout the nation, the most popular of which were the amusement parks. The parks were located in the countryside surrounding the cities, and to encourage ridership the companies waived admission fees for anyone who took their trolleys to the park. Americans were just learning to play, and amusement parks such as Coney Island in New York and Luna Park in Pittsburgh were

"Coney Island," stated the *New York Times* in 1892, "glorifies the scene of excitement our city [provides]." The largest of the many amusement parks built by the trolley companies, Coney Island featured roller coasters, a race track, camel and elephant rides, a canal, exhibition halls, and a huge beach area.

places of pure enchantment. "If Paris is France, then Coney Island, between June and September, is the world," wrote one 17-year-old visitor in a letter to her friend. One of Luna Park's earliest customers wondered, "What might the prophet have written in Revelation, if he had first beheld a spectacle like this."

Spectacles they were. The amusement parks, or trolley parks as they were also called, were filled with huge, brightly colored towers. Artificial lakes and waterfalls added to their allure. In the evening,

millions of electric lightbulbs, still a novelty at the time, illuminated every structure and dazzled all who entered the parks.

Visitors could purchase hot dogs, peanuts, popcorn, ice cream, and other treats. They could play games of chance and enjoy the rides, many of which

Throughout the country, tens of thousands of workers, like these men in New York City, found employment laying trolley tracks. The busy trolley business provided many new types of jobs.

were created specifically for the parks. Frightened yet delighted men, women, and children shrieked as they braved the roller coaster, the shoot-the-chutes, the bump-the-bump, and the Ferris wheel. For those not so adventurous, there were more sedate rides, such as the merry-go-round. Couples found the tunnel of love a special attraction. Young men were lured to the shooting galleries, where they could try to win a prize for their dates.

As the trolley parks grew and attracted millions of visitors, even more enticements were added. By the mid-1890s, many of the parks featured a swimming and boating area and a zoo. Some even installed a race-track. Motivated by the enormous success of the parks, trolley companies hired special managers whose job was to think of as many other reasons as they could for people to take the trolley.

Among the events and attractions these managers created were sightseeing parties, guided tours of the cities, family and veterans' reunions, band concerts, beach parties, lectures, office and factory outings, and visits to historic places—all dependent, of course, upon travel by trolley. At a time when baseball had established itself as the national pastime, trolley companies even organized baseball leagues and built diamonds and stadiums that thousands of spectators could conveniently reach by trolley.

The trolley companies also discovered that they could attract even more business by providing charter cars for those who could afford them. These cars, rented out for birthday parties and other special occasions, often had musicians and clowns aboard, along with an ice-cream chest and other features. Balloons and brightly colored Japanese lanterns decorated the cars.

All of these special activities attracted hundreds of thousands of riders, but other passengers enjoyed the trolley for the pure pleasure of the ride. The trolley provided urban dwellers with the most efficient way yet of escaping the crowds and the noise of the inner city for the glories of the countryside. Especially in the summer, millions of Americans left the city and enjoyed nature while riding in the special open-air summer

As more and more people traveled by trolley, new questions of etiquette arose. One question was whether men should give up their seats to women.

cars that almost all the trolley companies operated. The summer cars had their sides removed to let in the breezes and featured a large net at the front which shielded passengers from insects while the trolley was moving. Groups often chartered the summer trolleys for picnics and beach outings.

Some doctors considered trolley travel, particularly in the summer cars, to be beneficial for both body and mind. Earlier, some had blamed the nervous disorders of many city dwellers on the noise and hassles of omnibuses and horsecars. "Trolley cars," wrote one doctor in the *Boston Advertiser,* "travel fast enough to produce a feeling of mental exhilaration, which is absent from, or scarcely felt, by passengers in horsecars." Other physicians even proclaimed that riding in a trolley was the best of all cures for insomnia. They were convinced that a one-hour ride in an open-air trolley would almost always bring on a feeling of pleasant drowsiness.

Aside from their primary purpose of transporting people, trolleys were used for a wide variety of other purposes as well. In many cities, they served as rolling

Young women wearing skirts, like these students at a Brooklyn, New York, high school, learned how to board trolleys in a way that would not compromise their modesty.

mailboxes. A person could drop a letter into a passing streetcar, and the conductor would deposit the letter when the car passed by a post office. In some cities, special trolleys functioned as actual post offices. Painted a bright white and gold, these cars moved about the city picking up mail. Postal workers onboard the cars sorted the mail as quickly as it was picked up, reducing the time it took for a letter to be delivered.

Many cities utilized trolleys to carry out municipal services. These specially equipped streetcars hauled garbage, carried coal, and swept and watered down city streets. In Duluth, Minnesota, the city had a trolley fitted out to serve as a fire engine. Trolley cars were also specially designed to serve as hearses and funeral cars. The seats in a funeral trolley were upholstered in leather, and the windows were draped with black curtains. For the funeral of a prominent citizen, which would attract many mourners, several cars were coupled together to form a procession.

The trolley's role in revolutionizing the way people moved about the city was vital to the development of the United States. So, too, was the way it introduced Americans to recreation and leisure on a grand scale. And it was the trolley that created a type of community in which tens of millions of Americans still live—the suburb.

When cities began to feel overcrowded, public officials and private citizens looked at the surrounding countryside as a solution. If these open areas could be

"Always be on the lookout for youngsters attempting to steal a ride," the motorman's handbook warned its drivers in 1894. But keeping children from engaging in this dangerous practice was a challenge.

settled, overcrowding would be greatly reduced. The challenge was to find a way to transport large numbers of people between the two locales. The trolley provided the answer.

As the trolley companies extended their tracks beyond the cities in order to carry passengers to their amusement parks and other attractions, real estate developers began to build clusters of houses also easily reached by the trolleys. The cities, in turn, began to install sewers and other utilities in the suburbs, encouraging people to move into them. By the late 1890s, suburbs were springing up around cities throughout the nation and were becoming increasingly populated.

The suburbs offered the best of two worlds to its residents. Thanks to the trolley, families could live away from the noise, pollution, and frantic pace of the city but still enjoy its benefits. Husbands could wake up to the chirping of birds and then journey easily to their offices, factories, or stores. Wives could chat over the backyard fence with their neighbors and then travel into the city to do their shopping. Teenagers could commute daily to one of the many high schools or colleges that the city had to offer. At night, the entire family could enjoy the attractions of the city and then return comfortably to their quiet suburban dwelling.

It was not long before newspapers and other publications began proclaiming the virtues of the new way of life that the trolley and the suburbs made possible. The *New York Times* in 1893 stated:

> The trolley passing the door of [the businessman's] little country holding, delivers him, at a minimum cost, at the door of his factory or office in ample time to begin the day's work. And the same trolley car puts him down in his country dooryard for the evening meal with his family, which, in the meantime, has concerned itself with its garden, its sunshine, and its pure air.... The trolley is changing America, but nowhere more than in the manner in which it is moving [people] from country to city, and back again.

As the popularity of the trolley grew, its reach expanded. Soon, larger cars carrying more passengers even longer distances at greater speeds would crisscross the country.

Buses for Cities and Schools

Busses played a prominent role in the 1960s, when U.S. federal courts ordered cities to mix their racially segregated schools. School buses became a highly visible symbol of the attempts at desegregation.

The appearance of gasoline-powered automobiles in the first decade of the 1900s and the introduction of motorized buses shortly thereafter were major factors in the decline of the trolley. Today, the bus remains a vital method of transportation to millions of city dwellers, workers, and visitors. And in a nation where the vast majority of families own an automobile and millions own two or more, buses are a primary means of reducing city traffic.

One of the most common of all buses is the school bus. Like trolleys, the first school buses, which made their appearance in the late 1800s, were drawn by horses. With the development of the automobile these so-called "school wagons" were replaced by what were first known as "school trucks." During the 1920s and '30s, with the nation's roadway system expanding, particularly in rural areas, the need for vehicles to transport children to school increased and the school bus industry came into full flower. Since 1939, transportation experts from all the various states have met each year to develop new school bus safety standards. Today, more than 22 million students take the bus to school each day.

CHAPTER 4

The Incredible Interurbans

"A better way of seeing the country at reasonable cost
would be hard to imagine."

—E. C. Van Valkenburgh, reporter,
describing his 1,163-mile trip by interurbans, 1910

If the trolleys had been confined only to the cities and to the suburbs they created, they still would have represented a revolution in American transportation. But people far beyond the metropolitan areas felt their impact. As early as the beginning of the 1890s, trolley company owners came to the conclusion that if larger, faster, and even more comfortable vehicles than the streetcars could be built, people would be able to travel beyond the urban areas and from one city to another. To meet this need the interurban was soon developed, and it proved to be immensely popular.

Interurbans were much longer, larger, and heavier than trolleys. With motors of 50 to 160 horsepower (streetcar motors had 20 to 40 horsepower), interurbans could travel faster than 60 miles per hour in open country. Because of their weight, interurbans provided an even smoother ride than the trolley.

In several ways, interurbans were very much like trains. Most had a huge headlight, colored signal lights, and a loud whistle to warn of their approach. Like trains, interurbans ran on a set timetable and employed switchmen to control traffic at busy junctions.

Unlike trains, however, interurbans were powered by electricity rather than steam. While trains passed through the outskirts of cities, interurbans traveled through city streets much like a trolley, picking up speed once the city was left behind. And the interurbans needed no locomotives to pull them, which made them much less costly to operate and thus less expensive to ride.

The first interurban line in the United States, established in 1891, ran between Minneapolis and St. Paul, Minnesota. Two years later a line between Portland and Oregon City, Oregon, began operating. Like the trolleys that had spawned them, the interurbans were an instant success.

By 1900, lines had been established everywhere. "These great arteries are stimulating and benefiting to those sections of the country through which they pass," noted the *Street Railway Journal.* Nowhere was this more evident than in the nation's farming and rural areas, which had long been isolated from the advantages of the cities. Author Edith Wharton wrote in the *Berkshire Eagle* how the interurbans dramatically increased communication "between the scattered [Massachusetts] villages and the bigger towns in the valleys... [which] had libraries, theatres, and Y.M.C.A. halls to which the youth of the hills could descend for recreation." Some rural towns celebrated their new link to the wider world with a parade to greet the arrival of the first interurban.

By 1905, the interurban had become one of the most recognizable vehicles in the United States. In Ohio, for example, there was not a single community with more than 10,000 people that did not have interurban service. In the sprawling Los Angeles area, the Pacific Electric interurban system connected 42 cities and towns.

These vehicles were so admired that, like the nation's most fabled trains, they had specific names. In Indianapolis, Indiana, more than 7 million passengers a year traveled aboard the Muncie Meteor or the Marion

Many of the interurbans featured wide aisles with brightly lit interiors. Companies found that the long panels that ran along the sides of the cars were an excellent spot to advertise their goods.

Flyer. The names themselves symbolized the speed that the vehicles attained. As the interurban lines extended farther and farther out from the urban centers, people were able to travel great distances exclusively on the oversized trolleys. Passengers could make an uninterrupted journey, for example, between Indianapolis and Fort Wayne, Indiana (136 miles); Cleveland and Detroit (165 miles); or San Francisco and Chico, California (183 miles). A traveler could board an interurban in Youngstown, Ohio, and make the entire 440-mile trip to Jackson, Michigan, without changing cars.

And for those willing to change cars, the long-distance travel opportunities were even greater. By switching cars in New York, for example, a traveler could go all the way from Portland, Maine, to Sheboygan, Wisconsin, by interurban. By 1910, all but 187 of the 1,143 miles between Chicago and New York City were connected by interurban lines.

One of the most appealing features of long-distance interurbans like the Indiana Limited was their open rear porch, where passengers could watch the scenery as it whizzed by.

The popularity of the interurbans extended into Canada where, as in the United States, they helped bring people and places together. Because Canada's population was far more scattered than that of the United States, a limited number of interurban lines were built. The journey was often spectacular, however. One Canadian line, for example, crossed the international border on its route between Toronto and Buffalo, New York, and treated passengers to magnificent views of Niagara Falls and Lake Ontario.

Other Canadian lines stretched across that country's vast prairie. Two lines operated in the province of Manitoba and provided service out of Winnipeg. One of the most extensive of the Canadian interurban systems was established on the Pacific coast of British Columbia, with its main terminals located in Vancouver.

Traveling over such long distances required special types of accommodations, and in the United States, companies responded by making many of their cars as luxurious as possible. Chicago's North Shore line outfitted many of its interurbans with upholstered arm-chairs, radios, fans, and desks. The line also offered observation-parlor cars with a back porch from which, in mild weather, passengers could enjoy the fresh air and passing terrain. "A better way of seeing the country at reasonable cost would be hard to imagine," said the *Electric Railway Journal.* For long-distance trips, the North Shore line also ran what they called observation-buffet cars, which were staffed by a cook and two waiters.

The Illinois Traction System, on its route between Peoria, Illinois, and St. Louis, Missouri, featured cars that had small bedrooms with toilets, and sinks with hot and cold running water. Passengers who traveled on Chicago's South Shore line encountered sleeping cars as finely appointed as those on the most luxurious trains. In the dining cars, they feasted on steak, lobster, and venison, all served on the most elegant china. Many of the line's cars were constructed completely of steel, measured 60 feet long, and weighed 60 tons.

Not contented with the tens of millions of passengers they were already attracting, many interurban line owners followed the lead of earlier trolley magnates

Brill Dedenda Alarm Gong

THE Dedenda responds to each pressure on the pedal by a clear, penetrating note. There can be no chattering of the clapper as it is so constructed that it must rebound from the gong. Gongs come in 8, 12 and 14-in. sizes. Give thickness of crown piece.

This is an advertisement for a trolley alarm gong, which was used to signal stops and warn pedestrians. As trolleys became more numerous, many different kinds of companies were formed to supply the special equipment needed for the streetcars.

and built amusement parks where they could be easily reached by interurban. And just as the trolleys had spawned city suburbs, the interurbans also affected the nation's landscape. No matter how remote an area had once been, wherever interurbans regularly passed by, whole new towns sprang up, while existing towns grew larger and even became cities. In only 10 years, 17 new towns were founded along the tracks of Los Angeles's Pacific Electric line alone.

Travel by interurban became so popular that some authors found it highly profitable to create and publish what they called trolley guides. These guidebooks, with names such as *By Trolley through Western New England,* described various landscape features that passengers could see as the interurban traveled along a particular route. They also provided detailed descriptions of the historic homes and sites, restaurants, museums, and other places of interest in the surrounding areas. One guide explained,

> This booklet is published for the purpose of enabling one to learn what may be seen from the cars of different lines described, to tell you how to reach a given place, to record the mileage, running time, fare and such additional information as will contribute to one's ease of mind and pleasure.

Travelers found the guides to be extremely helpful. Some people used them to plan a vacation around traveling on the interurban from one destination to the next.

"We had been seized with trolley mania so long," wrote newlyweds Clinton and Louise Lucas, "that it was only natural that we should be carried away by it even on our honeymoon." Their trip was a 500-mile journey from Delaware to Maine. They kept a written record detailing all the places they visited, the ease with which they could leave one interurban and board another, and the many joys of what they called "rural trolleying." Later, their reminiscences were published in a book entitled *A Trolley Honeymoon*.

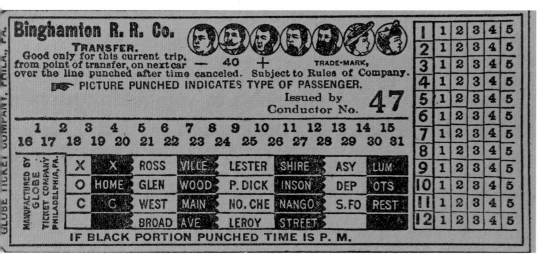

Interurban passengers were often given a transfer ticket that let them change cars and travel in a different direction without paying an additional fare. In order to prevent passengers from giving transfers to other riders, the tickets were printed with pictures of various types of people. The conductor would punch the appropriate picture when that customer first boarded the car.

Pack Square, looking East, Asheville, N. C.

Passengers board interurban cars in busy Pack Square
in this postcard from North Carolina. Most interurbans
began and ended their journeys in city squares.

CHAPTER 5

The Trolley Goes Underground

"The effect was like that when a barrier is removed from the channel

of a clogged river."

—*Boston Daily Globe* reporting on the
nation's first subway system, 1898

Although the interurbans continued to speed across America and the trolleys continued to crisscross the city landscapes, serious trouble lay ahead. Ironically, this trouble, as far as the trolleys were concerned, was linked directly to their success.

By the early 1900s, city streets, particularly in the downtown areas, were so filled with trolleys that the congestion reminded people of the days of uncontrolled horse-drawn traffic. Public officials now began to consider the possibility of building transportation systems beneath the ground as an answer to the problem.

The notion of developing an underground transportation system dates as far back as the Renaissance, an era from the 14th to the 17th century during which the arts and sciences flourished in Europe. In the mid-1500s, the streets of the city of Milan, Italy, were becoming so crowded that people could hardly move about. The artist and inventor Leonardo da Vinci suggested the city build underground thoroughfares to accommodate the traffic. Milanese officials, however, rejected the idea, and it would be 300 years before an underground transportation system would be constructed.

The world's first subway was built in London. Officially opened on January 10, 1863, this four-mile subterranean rail system was constructed only a few feet below the ground. By the end of the subway's first seven months of operation, more than 1.5 million passengers had traveled on it. In the following years, the London syubway system was greatly extended, and new lines were constructed within tubes that were sunk deep under the city streets.

Impressed with the immediate success of the London subway, transit promoters in America began pushing for the construction of similar systems. Transportation entrepreneur Hugh B. Wilson proposed building a subway under the streets of New York. "Our subway," according to Wilson's chief engineer,

> will signal the end of mud, dust, delays due to snow and ice. [It will mark] the end of a hazardous walk into the middle of the street to board the car, the end of waiting for lazy or obstinate [omnibus and horsecar drivers]. Everything will be out of sight, out of hearing. Nothing will indicate the thoroughfare below.

Wilson's plan had many supporters, but he faced a major obstacle that could not be overcome. At the time, almost all of New York politics was controlled by a single man named William Marcy ("Boss") Tweed, who had financial interests in both the omnibus and horsecar lines. Tweed knew that a subway would cut into his profits. When Wilson's proposal came before the New York legislature for approval, Tweed made certain that the legislators, most of whom he controlled, killed the plan.

In 1868, another New Yorker became determined to build a subway in his city. His name was Alfred Ely Beach, and the story of how he gave America its first, though ill-fated, subway reads like science fiction.

Beach was aware that his plan to bring underground transit to New York would, like Wilson's, be shot down by Boss Tweed. Already acclaimed for his invention of the world's first practical typewriter and the pneumatic tube, through which objects could be propelled by compressed air, Beach had a daring plan for getting around Tweed's opposition. He decided to

build an experimental subway that would run for a city block under Broadway, one of New York's busiest streets. Most important, Beach decided to build this first short section of track secretly, at night, under the cover of darkness.

Beach hoped that the enthusiastic response of passengers would be so overwhelming that the New York

Increasingly crowded city streets, such as this one in Buffalo, New York, motivated urban planners to build subways to take traffic underground.

legislature, despite its fear of Tweed, would have to vote him the money to extend his tracks into a full-fledged subway system. Beach knew that he had to find a place out of the public eye to dig his tunnel, so he rented the basement of a clothing store and had his construction crew haul the heavy digging equipment to the site. Every evening, as soon as it got dark, Beach, his son, and the crew dug their way through the earth, piling the dirt in the corners of the basement. After almost two years, they completed the task.

And they did much more. In order to make sure that the New York legislature was impressed, Beach and his workers constructed an elaborate, 120-foot-long station, where passengers could wait for the single car that would carry them along the short route. The station contained a working fountain, a grand piano, and paintings on the walls.

Beach's inventiveness did not stop with his construction methods. He devised a whole new way for the subway to be propelled. Rather than being pulled by a locomotive, Beach's car, which had no motor, fit tightly inside the tunnel and was blown along by an enormous steam-powered fan.

By February 1870, Beach was ready to demonstrate what he had created. He invited newspapermen and public officials to witness the first run along the subway that no one but he, his son, and the construction crew even knew existed. It caused a sensation. "Fashionable Reception Held in the Bowels of the Earth," exclaimed a headline in the *New York Herald*. Other newspapers heaped praise upon Beach's accomplishment and urged him to extend the subway line. Within weeks, some 400,000 intrigued passengers paid the 25¢ fare to ride the 312-foot-long experimental line.

Inspired by the response, Beach, who had spent $350,000 of his own money so far, appeared before the New York legislature and asked for the funds to extend his line. The legislators, also overwhelmed by what Beach had achieved, screwed up their courage and voted him the money. But Beach had underestimated the full extent of Boss Tweed's political power. The governor of New York, under Tweed's control, vetoed

Several ways of reducing city traffic were proposed in the years before the first subway was built in America. One plan that was never put into practice suggested that an arcade be built over New York's busy Broadway so that pedestrians and horse-drawn traffic could move freely above the trolley-filled street.

Inventor and magazine editor Alfred Beach secretly built 300 feet of subway track below Broadway in New York City. The luxurious car was propelled by giant fans and became a popular attraction.

the legislature's action. Beach's short tunnel, with his subway car still in it, was sealed up, and he died a disheartened man.

The first genuine American subway system appeared in Boston in 1896. By this time, new types of building materials and more effective ways of tunneling into the earth had been invented. Taking advantage of these advancements, the builders constructed a long, watertight tunnel of steel and concrete under the city's busiest streets. It was designed so that extensions of the system would be relatively easy to construct.

Boston's subway system opened to great fanfare in 1897. One of its features was the presence of ventilation shafts all along its route, which made the air in the tunnel fresher than that encountered by London's subway riders. Various Boston trolley lines were routed into the tunnel, particularly underneath the city's most heavily traveled areas. One of Boston's elevated lines also used the tunnel.

Cheers for the Nation's First Subway

Bostonians were filled with pride when, on September 1, 1897, the nation's first subway officially opened in that city. "First Car off the Earth" ran the banner headline in the *Boston Daily Globe.*

> Out of the sunlight of the morning and onto the white light of the subway rolled the first passenger carrying car at 6:01 A.M....Over 100 persons were aboard the car when it rolled down the incline leading to the [subway's opening] and they yelled themselves to the verge of apoplexy. Cheers were given for the motorman, for the conductor and for themselves.

Millions of people each year still ride the system's four main arteries: the Red Line, the Blue Line, the Orange Line, and the Green Line. Most are unaware of the specific reason for each of these colors. The Red Line originally ended at Harvard Square, and Harvard's official color is crimson. The Blue Line runs along the ocean. The Orange Line used to run beneath what was then called Orange Street. And the Green Line connects Boston with the leafy suburbs.

A brand-new trolley car travels through the just-opened Boston subway. On board are trolley conductors and subway officials taking a tour of the first permanent underground transportation system in the country.

Passengers in New York's 14th Street subway station
scurry along an underground platform. Deep beneath
the city streets, subways came to have a vitality of
their own.

Straphanging in the USA

Almost from the moment it began operating, the subway proved as effective in relieving the crush of city traffic in the streets above as its creators had hoped. "The effect was like that when a barrier is removed from the channel of a clogged river," claimed *The Boston Daily Globe* in 1897.

Boston's pioneering accomplishment paved the way for the construction of subway systems in other cities, such as Philadelphia, Cleveland, and Newark, New Jersey. By March 1900, Boss Tweed's political stranglehold on New York had been broken, and that city at last broke ground for its own subway system. Within a few decades, it would become the largest in the world.

At first, the tracks of most of the early subway systems, like the one in Boston, extended only under the most congested areas. Trolleys would travel along the streets, then enter the tunnel under a busy area, and then reemerge back on the streets. But as subway lines were increasingly extended over great distances, most began to run completely underground, and larger and faster cars were developed specifically for subway use.

One of the first modern subway systems, San Francisco's BART (Bay Area Rapid Transit) serves some 350,000 passengers each weekday. BART's underground areas feature well-lighted platforms and passageways, air conditioning, electronic signs, and escalators.

CHAPTER 6

Modern Rails for Modern Cities

"It is not my idea that there should be less ownership of automobiles, but that those who have no need for their cars for their daily activities should leave them at home, and avail themselves of public carrier facilities."

—Philip Harrington, Chicago commissioner of subways and superhighways, in a 1941 report to the Chicago city council

In addition to the subway, another invention appeared on the scene to threaten the use of the trolleys. Americans have always been looking for better ways to travel, and by the 1920s, millions were switching to automobiles and motor buses. The automobile took America by storm. Automobiles were not tied to tracks. They could go almost anywhere. People could travel at any time. No motorman or conductor was required. For millions, driving a car became a joy in itself. As more and more autos poured off the assembly lines, they increasingly took the place of trolleys and interur-

bans for family outings and errands. So many automobiles began to appear in the cities that some companies had to repaint their trolleys with bright colors so that fast-moving automobiles would not keep smashing into them.

Faced with a shrinking ridership—the result of passengers turning to both subways and automobiles—trolley owners tried to keep their companies alive by cutting costs and introducing cars that could carry more passengers. In 1916, the Birney car, named for its designer, Charles Birney, made its first appearance. The

Birney was much smaller than a standard-size trolley. It was designed so that the motorman could carry out all its operations, which saved the trolley company the expense of a conductor. More than 6,000 Birneys were manufactured, and they enjoyed a brief period of popularity. But the public soon tired of their dumpy appearance and of the uneven ride they provided.

A few cities attempted to combat the automobile invasion by ordering streetcars that could carry more passengers than any previously built trolley. The most noteworthy of these experiments took place in Detroit. The 140-seat car introduced in that city in 1924 was the largest streetcar in existence. It required a four-man crew and was usually filled to capacity at rush hours

"Carfare" to Los Angeles
—$51, or $9 Monthly?

Pacific Electric Railway
Largest Interurban Electric System in the World.

Advertisements like this one were designed to convince commuters that it was much less expensive to ride to work by trolley than by car. Trolley company owners did not give in to the automobile challenge without a fight.

when, ironically, it took automobile plant workers back and forth from work. But during the rest of the day, the enormous trolleys were less than half full.

One last effort to save the trolley proved to be a success and resulted in the production of the most streamlined and efficient streetcar ever to appear in the United States. By the early 1930s, the American Electric Railway Association, the governing body of the trolley systems, realized that individual efforts to save the trolleys were not succeeding. The association, however, had its own idea. It believed that the only way in which the trolleys could compete with the growing popularity of the automobile was through the design and production of the perfect streetcar.

To make its idea a reality, the association gathered together the top officials of 25 major trolley companies and convinced them to pool their resources to develop a trolley that passengers could not resist. These men banded together in a group called the Presidents' Conference Committee. The committee went about its work with a dedication worthy of its goal. It set up a testing site in Brooklyn, New York, designed to uncover every flaw in all the different kinds of trolleys in operation. Street railways from around the nation sent cars to be tested for such things as the volume and nature of the noise they produced and the amount and frequency of vibrations that passengers felt while riding in the cars.

The San Francisco bay is in the background as a cable car climbs one of the city's many steep slopes.

These and other design and performance tests and experiments were carried out for five years. The result was the PCC car (named for the committee), which has been described by transportation experts as one of the most outstanding achievements in the history of public urban transportation. The all-steel PCCs were lightweight and more streamlined in appearance than any previous streetcars. For passenger comfort, they featured cushioned seats and a vastly improved heating system. Their motors were so quiet that they could hardly be heard. Perhaps most startling of all was that the brakes never screeched, unlike any trolleys that had ever been built. PCCs were such a success that within five years of their first appearance on the streets of Brooklyn in 1935, more than 1,100 of the vehicles were being used in cities throughout the United States. The American Electric Railway Association had proved its point. It had been possible to create a streetcar so marvelous that it would rekindle the nation's interest.

Even so, the PCC could not stem the nation's growing love affair with the automobile. Nor could it blunt the effect of the large-city subway systems, which also lured away former street railway riders. By the 1960s, only nine of all the hundreds of North American cities that had once had teeming trolley systems still had streetcars in operation. Interestingly, these eight cities—Boston, Cleveland, Newark, New Orleans, Philadelphia, Pittsburgh, San Francisco, and Toronto—still have trolley service, in one form or another, in operation today.

As far back as 1941, Chicago transportation official Philip Harrington stated,

> It would undoubtedly be the ideal standard of travel if every one were able and could afford to execute all his movements in his own car, with complete safety, free from all traffic annoyance and delay and have a doorman take and deliver the car whenever the need for parking arose.... But we know that no such traffic Utopia is possible.... It is not my idea that there should be less ownership of automobiles, but that those who have no need for their cars for their daily activities should leave them at home, and avail themselves of public carrier facilities.

The Seattle Center Monorail is the nation's first full-scale monorail system. A favorite part of the Seattle skyline, the monorail links downtown Seattle to outlying attractions such as the Space Needle and the Pacific Science Center.

Since the 1970s, urban transit experts and public officials have sought to develop new types of transportation systems to eliminate traffic congestion and to make travel within and between cities as efficient and convenient as possible. Some of these experts believe that the answer lies in the building of monorail systems. These streamlined cars straddle and move at extremely high speeds along a single elevated rail. Millions of people have ridden the short monorails at Disneyland and Walt Disney World. Millions of others have traveled along the one-mile monorail in Seattle, Washington, which was originally constructed in 1962 to serve visitors to that city's world's fair. But to date no monorail system of significant length has been built in the United States.

One advanced modern urban transportation system that has been highly successful, however, is the 95-mile San Francisco system known as BART (Bay Area Rapid Transit). BART's automated, aerodynamically designed cars travel at up to 80 miles per hour over rails that take them through some 19 miles of subways and tunnels, 23 miles of aerial track, and some 53 miles of surface rails. Each weekday BART transports some 350,000 passengers. Since its opening in September 1972, it has carried more than 1.5 billion riders over more than 18 billion miles. During commuter rush hours in the heavily populated area it serves, BART is 10 times more energy efficient than automobiles.

BART was developed in the 1970s, along with a whole new type of urban rail system that many transportation experts regard as the real future of urban transit. It is called "light rail," and it is an electric railway system characterized by its ability to operate single or multiple trolley-like cars on railed streets, on aerial structures, or in subways. As modern transportation supporter Jim Seamon has defined it, "Light rail is the child of a streetcar mother and a rapid transit father. It is a nephew to an interurban line, a cousin to the commuter rail, and a step-brother to a bus."

The term "light rail" is actually a misnomer, since light rail cars are as heavy as the old-time trolleys. But because they are capable of traveling underground,

Thanks to computer technology, most cities have replaced tokens and tickets with electronic fare cards. The cards, like this one from the Miami-Dade, Florida light rail system, are easier for passengers to carry and are a more efficient way to keep track of the number of riders and the amount of fares collected every day.

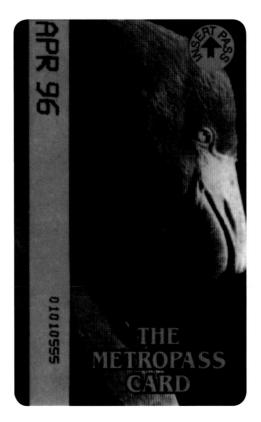

above the ground, or at street level, they provide one of the best answers yet to alleviating urban traffic congestion. Other advantages include their ability to cope with steep grades and tight curves, their large passenger capacity (up to 250 people per car), and the comfortable, smooth ride they provide. For all these reasons, as well as the fact that they are relatively inexpensive to install and maintain, light rail systems have been built in American cities from Buffalo, New York, to San Diego, California.

Ironically, San Francisco, the same city that has provided the nation with its most successful modern urban transportation system, is also famous for its widespread use of the cable car, a vehicle that dates back almost to the very beginnings of the trolley. Today, some 130 years after Andrew Hallidie successfully tested the first cable car in that city, one of San Francisco's main attractions are the 40 cable cars that transport both tourists and residents within the city.

Throughout the 1900s, San Francisco's cable cars were a constant source of controversy among its residents. Many questioned the expense involved in maintaining a system that had long been abandoned by every other American city. But thousands of other citizens demanded that the city retain the cable cars that had become a symbol of San Francisco. "The cable cars were here when this town was really magic," wrote columnist Herb Caen in the *San Francisco Chronicle*. "We look upon them now

With the help of sophisticated computers, a Dallas, Texas, light rail employee keeps track of the many cars in the system. Inaugurated in 1996, Dallas's light rail system now extends for more than 20 miles, includes 20 stations, and carries more than 28,000 passengers every day.

with adoring eyes. They can do no wrong. [They] cost us a fortune, but without them we'd be lost." In the years leading up to the early 1980s various lines of the system were shut down for financial reasons. But in 1984, Caen and his fellow cable car proponents rejoiced when, accompanied by parades and other fanfare, full cable car service was restored.

Today, 40 cable cars carry nearly 10 million passengers through the streets of San Francisco every year and reduce the number of automobiles on the streets. They also provide a vivid reminder of the days when the trolley in its various forms not only moved city dwellers about with ease but forever changed the American landscape.

The trolley made inexpensive mass urban transportation possible. It built the amusement parks and created the suburbs. The interurbans connected the cities, spawned new towns, and made overland travel itself a form of recreation. But there were other, less obvious accomplishments as well.

Trolleys and interurbans revolutionized farmers' lives, making it easier for them to sell their products and ending their isolation. They made it possible for the well-to-do to build country homes. And by bringing together people of different economic means, they served as a unifying force, easing tensions between various groups.

The trolleys and interurbans provided travelers, city dwellers, and commuters with transportation that was inexpensive, dependable, and safe. And they were pollution-free. Today, in fact, many transportation and environmental experts are seriously calling for their return.

Just like the original trolleys, the cars in the Cleveland, Ohio, light rail system are powered by electricity and run on tracks not separated from regular traffic.

Timeline

1831
First omnibus line is established

1832
First horsecar line is established

1844
Boston, Philadelphia, and New York establish omnibus lines

1868
First section of New York's elevated railway is completed

1870
Alfred Ely Beach demonstrates his short subway tunnel

1872
Devastating horse disease spreads throughout the American East

1873
Andrew Hallidie introduces cable railway in San Francisco

1887
First electrically powered street railway system

1890–1910s
Trolley companies establish amusement parks

1891
First interurban line is established

1897
First American subway system

1900
Construction begins on New York City's subway system

1910
Interurban lines connect all but 187 of the 1,143 miles between Chicago and New York

1924
Largest streetcar in existence (140 seats) goes into service

1962
Seattle Monorail opens

1972
San Francisco's Bay Area Rapid Transit (BART) system begins operations

1973
New York City's Third Avenue El is torn down

1990
Light Rail service begins in Los Angeles, California

2002
Construction of light rail systems begins in Camden, New Jersey; Cincinnati, Ohio; Houston, Texas; and Minneapolis/St. Paul, Minnesota

Places to Visit

There are transit museums throughout the United States where you can view vintage trolleys, learn about the history of specific trolleys and trolley lines, and come face to face with artifacts related to the trolley era. Many of these museums also offer visitors trolley rides.

California

San Francisco Cable Car Museum
1201 Mason Street
San Francisco, CA 94108
415-929-1873
www.cablecarmuseum.com

Connecticut

Connecticut Trolley Museum
58 North Road
East Windsor, CT 06088
860-627-6540
www.ceraonline.org

Illinois

Fox River Trolley Museum
361 South LaFox Street
   (Illinois Route 31)
South Elgin, IL 60177
847-697-4676
www.foxtrolley.org

Maine

Seashore Trolley Museum
195 Log Cabin Road
Kennebunkport, ME 04046
207-967-2712
www.trolleymuseum.org

Maryland

National Capitol Trolley Museum
1313 Bonifant Road
Colesville, MD 20905
301-384-6088
www.dctrolley.org

Minnesota

Minnesota Transportation Museum
193 Pennsylvania Avenue E
St. Paul, MN 55101
800-711-2591
www.mtmuseum.org

New York

New York Transit Museum
Boerum Place and Schermerhorn
   Street
Brooklyn, NY 11201
718-694-5100
www.mta.nyc.us/museum

North Carolina

Charlotte Trolley Museum
2104 South Boulevard
Charlotte, NC 28203
704-375-0850
www.charlottetrolley.org

Pennsylvania

Pennsylvania Trolley Museum
1 Museum Road
Washington, PA 15301
877-728-7655
www.pa-trolley.org

Further Reading

Appelgate, Ray D. *Trolleys and Streetcars on American Picture Postcards.* New York: Dover, 1979.

Bourne, Russell. *Americans on the Move.* Golden, Colo.: Fulcrum, 1995.

Cavin, Ruth. *Trolleys: Remembering the Electric Interurban Railways.* New York: Dutton, 1976.

Demorro, Harre and John Harder. *Light Rail Transit on the West Coast.* New York: Quadrant, 1989.

Fischler, Stanley. *Moving Millions: An Inside Look at Mass Transit.* New York: Harper & Row, 1985.

————. *Uptown, Downtown. A Trip through Time on New York's Subways.* New York: Hawthorn/Dutton, 1979.

Fletcher, Ken. *Centennial State Trolleys: The Life and Times of Colorado's Streetcars.* Denver: Colorado Railroad Historical Foundation, 1995.

Middleton, William D. *Time of the Trolley: The Street Railway from Horsecar to Light Rail.* San Marino, California: Golden West Books, 1987.

Miller, John. *Fares, Please! A Popular History of Trolleys, Horse-Cars, Street-Cars, Buses, Elevated, and Subways.* New York: Dover Publications, 1960.

Reidman, Sarah. *Clang! Clang! The Story of Trolleys.* New York: Rand McNally, 1991.

Rowsome, Frank. *Trolley Car Treasury.* New York: McGraw-Hill, 1956.

Sandler, Martin W. *This Was America.* Boston: Little, Brown, 1980.

Sullivan, Fred, and Fred Winkowski. *Trolleys of North America.* New York: Motorbooks International, 1995.

Yepsen, Roger. *City Trains: Moving Through America's Cities by Rail.* New York: Macmillan, 1993.

Index

Page numbers in italics indicate illustrations.

Acknowledgments

I wish to thank Carol Sandler for all the help and encouragement she has given me. Thanks are also due to Karen Fein for her valuable aid and to Alexis Siroc for creating such an appealing design for the book. Finally, I am grateful for having Nancy Hirsch as my editor. Her editing skills are but part of the many contributions she has made to this book.

Picture Credits

Martin W. Sandler is the author of more than 40 books. His *Story of American Photography: An Illustrated History for Young People* received the Horn Book Award in 1984. Sandler's other books include *America, A Celebration!, Photography: An Illustrated History, The Vaqueros: The World's First Cowmen,* and the Library of Congress American history series for young adults. An accomplished television producer and writer as well, Sandler has received Emmy and Golden Cine awards for his television series and programs on history, photography, and American business. He has taught American studies to students in junior high and high school, as well as at the University of Massachusetts and Smith College. He lives in Cotuit, Massachusetts, with his wife, Carol.

Other titles in the Transportation in America series include:

Galloping across the USA: Horses in American Life

On the Waters of the USA: Ships and Boats in American Life

Riding the Rails in the USA: Trains in American Life

Driving around the USA: Automobiles in American Life

Flying over the USA: Airplanes in American Life